# BOURNE to SAXBY

by

John Rhodes

*The ornate wooden shelters at Saxby station, photographed on the occasion of a visit by King Edward VII (and dog) in January 1907. The Bourne-Saxby line is in the foreground. (Lens of Sutton)*

KMS BOOKS, BOSTON

First published in 1989

 Look out for further titles in this series to be published in the future.

CONTENTS

Chapter One - Developments at Bourne & Saxby ................. page 4

Chapter Two - The Bourne - Saxby Link .......................... page 8

Chapter Three - Construction & Opening .......................... page 11

Chapter Four - The Route .......................................... page 21

Chapter Five - Early Goods Traffic & Passenger Workings....... page 29

Chapter Six - Decline & Closure .................................. page 38

Bourne - Saxby : Main Dates ...................................... page 48

Publisher - KMS Books
Assembly Rooms, Market Place,
Boston, Lincs. PE21 6LY
Telephone: (0205) 311111

ISBN 0 948017 07 4

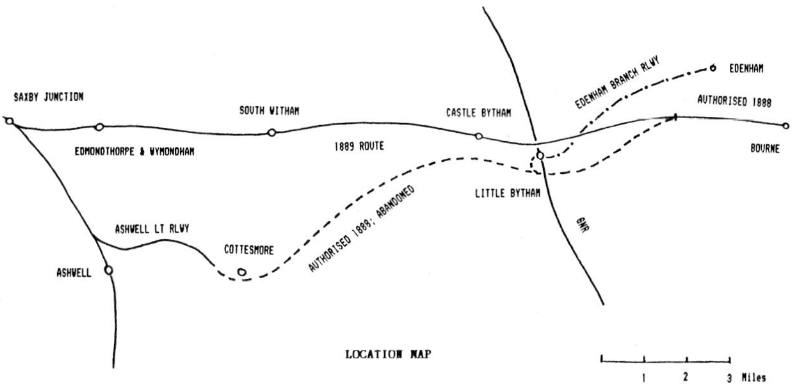


LOCATION MAP

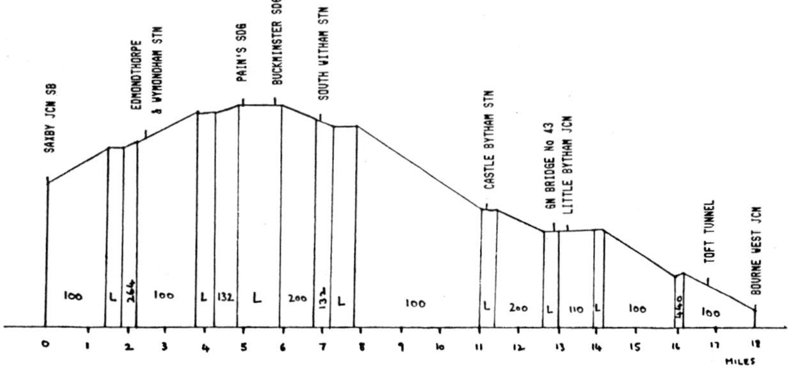


GRADIENT PROFILE: SAXBY-BOURNE

# CHAPTER ONE
# DEVELOPMENTS AT BOURNE AND SAXBY

## SAXBY

In the mid 1840s, the wily and unscrupulous George Hudson was at the height of his powers. As manager of the newly-formed Midland Railway he controlled over 1,000 miles of actual railway and was prodigiously inventive in his schemes for further proposed railways: in the space of two days in May 1846 he received approval for 40 different railway bills, with a total capital of ten million pounds. Nicknamed 'The Railway King' in tribute to his empire-building talents, he wielded immense influence locally and nationally, and he had amassed a personal fortune large enough to enable him to live an appropriately regal lifestyle. By a formidable blend of bluster, financial juggling and double dealing that amounted to genius, he had so far managed to out-manoeuvre most attempts from rival Companies to trespass on what he regarded as his Company's sphere of influence and area of operation. The proposal for a direct line between York and London by a Company which later emerged as the Great Northern, however, presented Hudson with a big problem. If the line were authorised, it would undoubtedly pose a serious threat to his own York-London route, which ran via the Midlands and was a rather circuitous way of reaching the capital. Faced with the prospect of major loss of traffic, Hudson turned his energies to countering, blocking and discrediting the rival scheme in an attempt to wreck it totally, and although he managed to delay the GN plans for a time, he ultimately failed, of course, to prevent their authorisation. The various ingenious, and sometimes underhand, ways in which he tried to stave off the opposition are irrelevant to this study, except for one scheme which brought a railway line to, among other places, the remote and insignificant village of Saxby, in Leicestershire.

In 1845 the Eastern Counties Railway, of which Hudson was later to become Chairman, had been authorised to build a line westwards from Ely to the cathedral city of Peterborough, and Hudson recognised that an alliance between his own Midland Railway and the ECR would be useful in pre-empting the London-York proposals by securing traffic from the Peterborough area before the London-York Company reached there. Accordingly, Hudson put forward proposals for a railway from Peterborough, via Stamford, Oakham and Melton Mowbray, to Syston, where it would join the Midland line into Leicester. The route was sanctioned on June 30, 1845, but not before it had encountered some fierce and implacable opposition from a not entirely unexpected quarter.

Some miles north of Oakham, close to the village of Saxby, lay Stapleford Hall, the stately home of Lord Harborough. It was here that Hudson's route swung through ninety degrees to turn due west, skirting as it did so the extensive parkland, nearly a thousand acres, in which the Hall stood. Lord Harborough, a rather tetchy and irascible aristocrat, had for some time been a major shareholder in the Oakham Canal Company, which in 1802 had opened the 15-mile waterway from a junction with the Melton Mowbray Navigation to the town of Oakham. The canal's principal traffic was coal inwards and agricultural produce outwards, and even though it was always a shaky proposition financially, it did provide a useful service for the Earl's own estates, since there were wharves at both Saxby and Stapleford for the loading and unloading of goods. Lord Harborough's financial interest in the canal meant that he was inherently suspicious of railways, which were already beginning to kill off canal traffic up and down the country, and when he became aware that Hudson's proposed railway route not only ran in close proximity to his own stately home, but also intended to link the towns of Oakham and Melton Mowbray, which were already served by the canal, he was stung into active opposition.

The first moves in what was to become known as the Battle of Saxby came in November 1844, when seven of Hudson's surveyors arrived in the Stapleford area to reconnoitre the route and take the necessary measurements and levels of the land. Lord Harborough had already festooned the borders of his property with large notices threatening dire retribution on anybody attempting to enter his park for surveying purposes, and he backed up his threats by posting groups of estate workers at strategic points along his boundaries. As they approached the Park, the Midland surveyors were confronted by nine or ten of Lord Harborough's men, armed with pitchforks and sticks, and ordered away, even though they were still on public land. When they refused to turn back, they were set upon, herded into a farm cart, and driven off to the local magistrate. Since the Midland men had committed no crime, however, there was no legal action that could be taken against them, and the Earl's head keeper had to be content with venting his annoyance against them by tipping them out of the cart into the road. The surveyors were made of stern stuff, however, and, bruised but undaunted, returned the next day, prudently bringing with them a sizeable contingent of brawny navvies, borrowed from local railway workings, and some equally hefty prize-fighters imported from Nottingham. Lord Harborough's men, their numbers also reinforced, met them head-on, and a spectacular melee occurred as both groups shoved and pushed, crashed struggling into hedgerows, rolled furiously fighting in the mud of the roadway, or slid in a wild tangle of arms and legs into a dirty roadside ditch. The Midland contingent was eventually put to flight in a stirring chase along the canal towpath, to the cheers and excitement of a crowd of locals who had gathered to see the fun. Violence escalated again a couple of days later in another unseemly brawl, during which a gigantic lock-keeper, hired by Lord Harborough, single-handedly knocked unconscious half a dozen opponents and smashed a valuable piece of surveying equipment said to be worth £32. The end product of all this mayhem was jail sentences for several navvies on a charge of riot, fines for some of Lord Harborough's men for damage they had caused, and a postponement of surveying activities in the Stapleford Park area until tempers had cooled.

Even after the MR had gained Parliamentary approval for its route in June 1845, Lord Harborough stubbornly refused to allow any construction work to be started anywhere near his estate. Tactfully, the MR agreed to re-route its line a little further away from Stapleford Hall, but when the surveyors arrived, with a bodyguard, to take new measurements and levels they were once again confronted by a group of Lord Harborough's men and the second Battle of Saxby was soon in full swing. Lord Harborough himself enlivened the proceedings on this occasion by driving his carriage, Boadicea-like, into the ranks of the hated railwaymen. The surveying did eventually get done, and the deviation was authorised on June 16, 1846, with the provision for a tunnel to be driven underneath a spinney of fine trees, Cuckoo Plantation, on Lord Harborough's estate so that the offending trains would be hidden from his Lordship's view. Unfortunately, during construction the tunnel collapsed, causing subsidence to the trees and apoplexy to their aristocratic owner. There followed a sharp legal battle, which ended in yet another deviation proposal authorised on July 22, 1847. By this time, the two sections of line on either side of the Saxby area had already been built and were in operation, that from Syston to Melton from September 1, 1846, and from Peterborough to Stamford from October 2 of the same year. Because of Lord Harborough's intransigence, it was not until May 1, 1848 that these two sections were linked, and the whole through route in operation.

At Saxby, a small station was built on the western end of the much contested curve, just off the main road and about half a mile from the village, almost on the bank of the Oakham Canal. The MR had agreed to buy the canal in April 1845 for the sum of £26,000 and 200 new Midland £40 shares, a decision the canal authorities (Lord Harborough excepted) were happy to accept since traffic was clearly on the wane: in the very dry summer of 1844 the waterway had been unnavigable for five months and goods had to be transported laboriously by road.

By the 1880s, when train speeds had increased considerably, the severe curve at Saxby was proving something of a restriction, particularly to express services, and the MR decided to re-route the line yet again in order to ease the situation. By this time there was a new incumbent at Stapleford Hall, who proved much more amenable than his peppery predecessor, and the MR was able to obtain approval for a new curve, of 56 furlongs 3 chains radius, on June 24, 1889, by the same Act that sanctioned most of the Bourne-Saxby extension, detailed later in this book.

## BOURNE

The first railway to reach the small market town of Bourne, on the edge of the Fens, was the short 6-miles terminal branch from the Great Northern main line at Essendine. The enterprise was a product of local initiative, organised by the vicar of Bourn and a retired Army general, who, together with a group of local worthies and landowners, formed the Bourn & Essendine Railway Company in 1857. The line opened, to the celebratory ringing of church bells, in May 1860, but was always under financial pressure, and was soon taken over the GNR, which had operated the route from the beginning. Modest in scale the line might have been, but it did boast at its Bourne end a fine station building, the Red Hall, a former Elizabethan manor house thought at one time to have associations with the Gunpowder Plot (a claim recently shown to have been false), and which had passed through various ownerships, eventually becoming a private school for young ladies in the years immediately before the B & E took it over for use as station offices. A service of six passenger trains a day each way meant that Bourne was now in vital contact with the rest of the country, with easy access to London and the north, and with the benefit of cheaper coal and other goods being brought in, and agricultural produce going out to wider markets than was possible before.

Communications for the town improved even more a few years later, in 1866, when the Spalding & Bourn Railway reached there from the east, by a virtually dead straight, and single-track line which gave access to the junction station at Spalding, where routes from Peterborough, Boston, Lincoln and South Lynn converged. On January 2 1872, the GN opened passenger operations (5 trains a day each way) along a 17-mile branch from Bourne northwards to Sleaford, an event that was also celebrated by church bells ringing and large crowds of sightseers gathering at intermediate stations to cheer the first trains on their way. Thus, within a dozen years, Bourne had become an important railway junction, with something like 30 passenger trains a day, and a steady stream of freight to all parts of the country.

Station facilities had developed correspondingly to keep pace with the growth in traffic. The original B & E station had consisted of a single short platform in front of Red Hall; there was also a small engine and carriage-shed combined, a coal siding, and a 2-road goods yard. The arrival of the Spalding & Bourn had turned the station from a terminus into a through route, so an additional, island, platform was added (the Red Hall platform, being extended at the same time to double its length) and a third small platform, for the use of S & B trains only, added adjacent to South Street level crossing (although this probably only lasted for a few months). Siding space was increased and a new engine shed built. The S & B also had its own goods yard and shed to east of South Street. The opening of the Sleaford branch necessitated the installation of a signal box to control the junction, and a turntable was added to the engine-shed facilities.

By the 1870s, then, railway routes extended north, south and east from Bourne; as yet, however, there was no direct access available westwards, to give a link with the Midlands. It was possible to reach Nottingham via Essendine and Grantham, but this was something of a roundabout route and involved a change of trains at Essendine. A connection between Bourne and the MR Syston-Peterborough line would provide the best and most direct route, and it was, accordingly, in this direction that the next moves were made during the 1880s.

# CHAPTER TWO

# THE BOURNE- SAXBY LINK.

Although it was only in the last decade of the century that the Bourne-Saxby link was finally realised, it had been mooted as a viable proposition as far back as 1864, as part of the proposals for the line which eventually materialised as the Bourne-Spalding railway. The opening of that line in 1866 provided the link in a railway route that joined the GN main line at Essendine, via Bourne and Spalding, to Sutton Bridge and South Lynn in Norfolk. As yet, however, there was no possibility of through running since the component parts of the link were owned by four separate Companies: the GN (Essendine-Bourne); the Spalding & Bourn; the Norwich & Spalding (Spalding-Sutton Bridge); and the Lynn & Sutton Bridge. Two of these Companies, the Spalding & Bourn and the Lynn & Sutton Bridge, proposed an amalgamation into a new Company to be called the Midland & Eastern, which would then lease the Norwich & Spalding and build a new extension westwards from Bourne to join the MR at Saxby, thus linking the eastern counties and the Midlands by a more direct route than was then available. The MR, recognising an opportunity to extend its influence into GN territory, was quick to give its support to the scheme; the GN, seeing the Midland threat, was equally swift to oppose it. The conflict was resolved, when the Bill reached the Committee stage in the Commons, by a compromise between the two major Companies in which the Midland agreed to withdraw its support for the Saxby extension proposal in return for running powers over GN metals from Bourne to Essendine and from there, over a route then under construction, to Stamford, where a junction could be effected with the Midland's own Peterborough-Syston line. The formal agreement was ratified on July 1, 1866, and the first Bourne-Saxby link was thereby dropped, to lie in abeyance for more than 20 years.

The idea was resurrected in 1888 by the Eastern & Midland, a Company formed by takeover of all the smaller Companies formerly controlling the lines between Bourne and Lynn. Again in collaboration with the MR, the E & M proposed a line westwards from Bourne via Witham-on-the-Hill, crossing the GN main line south of Little Bytham station (where there would be a connecting junction) and then looping round to take in the villages of Clipsham, Stretton and Greetham before making an end-on junction with the existing MR mineral branch line at Cottesmore (see Location Map). Iron-ore had been quarried in this area since 1882, the ore at first being carried by horse and cart the couple of miles to Ashwell station, on the MR's Peterborough-Syston line, but the Midland soon found it more convenient to open a railway branch line to the edge of the ore field, where a network of tramways then led off into the quarries themselves. Since this branch was already laid to standard gauge, it would have been a simple operation to upgrade the track and adapt it for passenger working in order for it to become part of the through route to Bourne.

In return for Midland support of the scheme, the E & M agreed to route as much traffic as possible via the MR, rather than via the GNR from Bourne to Essendine, a proposal that was once again vigorously contested by the GN. Although the line received authorisation on June 28, 1888, the traffic agreement was thrown out by the Commons Committee and, again inevitably, the Companies concerned re-thought their positions and arrived at a compromise solution. The decision was made by the two large Companies, the MR and GNR, since the E & M was by this time sliding into deep financial trouble; the proposal was for a new route west from Bourne to cross the GN main line north of Little Bytham station (with, as before, a connecting junction) and then via South Witham to a junction at Saxby. The line would be under joint MR/GNR control from Bourne as far as Little Bytham (a double-track section), while the remaining, single-line, section would belong exclusively to the Midland. Plans for the new line (and also for the new, less severe, curve at Saxby, mentioned earlier) were drawn up by Alfred Langley, the Midland's engineer, and deposited on November 28, 1888, in order to meet the requirements for consideration in the 1889 Parliamentary session.

No problems were encountered in the Bill's progress and it passed smoothly through all stages, receiving sanction on June 24, 1889. By this time it was obvious that the E & M's financial problems were insuperable, and in 1891 the MR and GNR made an offer to take over the E & M route jointly, and, after some negotiation, this offer was accepted. The new Committee of the M & GN Joint took control of the E & M system from July 1, 1893, by which date the Bourne-Saxby line had been opened to goods traffic and trains were running between the Midlands and Spalding, Lynn and the eastern counties. This, however, is to anticipate events a little; the next chapter backtracks a few years to detail the construction of the line itself.

*Red Hall, the original Bourne & Essendine station building, before the 1893 conversion. The platform ramp, later removed to make way for two sidings, can just be seen in the left foreground (Welholme Galleries)*

# CHAPTER THREE
# CONSTRUCTION AND OPENING

The 18 miles of line, construction of which was under the overall charge of J. Allen McDonald, the Midland's Chief Engineer, were divided into three sections, and tenders invited accordingly. Eventually, the contract for the first section, Saxby to South Witham, including the new Saxby curve, was awarded to the firm of Hulme & King, of London and Liverpool, with Mr. A. Wilson as their resident engineer; the middle section, from South Witham to Little Bytham, was given to Messrs. J.W. Nowell of Manchester, an old-established firm of railway contractors who had worked on the London & Birmingham line as far back as the late 1830s; and the final section, Little Bytham to Bourne, was taken by William Mousley of Eccleshall, Staffordshire, whose resident engineer was George McDonald. Mousley's firm was also awarded the contract for the new station at Bourne, and for the Spalding avoiding line, both being built at the same time. All contracts had been let by October 1890, when work was able to get under way along the route.

*The signpost at Little Bytham Junction marking the point at which the Joint and Midland lines met end to end. (E.L. Back)*

On the Saxby section, the first contract to be awarded, work had got off to a brisk start; by the beginning of November several miles of single line had already been laid. The track, in 30' lengths, was 85lbs to the yard, joined with plain fishplates wedged into 50lbs chairs, and ballasted mostly with broken stones and ashes. The land rose steadily between Saxby and a point mid-way between Wymondham and South Witham, where the summit of the line was reached, and a good deal of embanking and cutting was necessary to maintain workable gradients: the new Saxby curve and the junction with the Bourne line were carried on a 700-yard long embankment over a tributary of the River Eye, and there were two sizeable cuttings, one half a mile long, between Saxby and Wymondham.

On the middle section, six miles of route, work was under way by October 1890. South Witham became the headquarters of the navvy work-force, and a large settlement soon sprang up on the edge of the village, in a field belonging to a Mr Cooper, conveniently close to the Blue Bull public-house. Workshops for carpenters and blacksmiths were erected, equipped with a circular saw and a mortar-mill, both driven by steam power; a well was sunk to provide water for the engines. About a hundred men, divided into three groups, were employed on embanking work and shifting material, which was done initially by horse and cart. Stone for building work was dug from a local quarry in Mill Lane. Bad weather hampered progress at the beginning of December, when heavy snow made it necessary to suspend operations and lay off, albeit temporarily, a large number of navvies; by Christmas, however, conditions had eased and in order to make up for lost time the contractors, Messrs. Nowell (an aptly seasonal name) brought in digging machinery in the form of a Dunbar & Ruston "steam navvy". Steam-driven excavating machines were not new - the American railroad builders had been using them since the 1840s - but it was not until the end of the century that contractors in this country began to use them in any numbers. One machine, it was estimated, could do the work of between 30 and 80 men, and give a saving of up to 1/- a cubic yard of material removed. In such a quiet and remote rural area as South Witham, a steam navvy was a distinct novelty, and crowds of locals regularly turned out to gawp at the snorting monster biting its way through the countryside at a rate of 1,000 cubic yards a day.

The section between Little Bytham and Bourne was the most difficult on the route, and offered the most severe challenge to the contractor. The land to the east of Bourne is fenland, stretching out totally level for 25 miles until it reaches the waters of the Wash. West of the town, however, the terrain rises in a series of ridges, none of them spectacularly steep but between them combining to climb from a mere 35' above sea level to a high point of 439' between Wymondham and South Witham. The escarpment which overlooks Bourne was too steep to allow the line to be taken over it and so a tunnel had to be driven through it; even so, the line was still forced to climb at a steady 1 in 100 for four miles beyond the station with only a slight stretch falling at 1 in 440 at the halfway stage. Preliminary work on the tunnel started in November 1890 with the sinking of two shafts; for a depth of 50' the excavators worked through shale, but then struck hard rock, which slowed progress appreciably and necessitated the use of gunpowder to loosen it. At the other end of the section, however, round Little Bytham, work was carried on at a good rate, although the December snowstorms caused a similar laying-off of workmen here as at South Witham. Notwithstanding, the Chief Engineer was so satisfied with overall progress that by the end of the year it was being confidently forecast that the whole line would be ready for operation by August 1892.

1891 saw very solid progress made along the whole route. Tunnelling work got under way in earnest at the beginning of February, with the initial work-force of 100 men soon increased to about 400, most of them housed in a shanty settlement of temporary wooden huts. An order for one million of the two and a half million bricks needed for lining the tunnel was placed with the local brickmaker, Henry Kingston of Bourne, who made the bricks from clay dug from the foot of Stamford Hill, through which the tunnel was to be driven, where deposits lay 12' deep. A whole collection of workshops - a saw-mill, mortar-mill, smithies and carpenters shops - grew up around the workings. The tunnel shafts were served by two winding engines, while the air below was kept tolerably fresh by the use of a Roots patent blower to ventilate the excavations. Water was supplied at the site of operations by one and a quarter mile length of pipe fed by a bore-hole at Bourne. Spoil removed from the tunnel and from the cutting at its east end was taken to Spalding to form the embankment for the new loop line being built there; four trains of 20 wagons each made the journey every day, carrying between them 400 cubic yards of earth.

In order to facilitate the conveyance of material, such as bricks, from Bourne to the work-face, a two and a half mile tramway was laid to serve not only the tunnel but also the viaduct over the Glen valley at Lound, a little further down the line, work on which started in October 1891. The bridge was of five arches, each of 40' span and 44' from ground to rail level, and required one and a half million bricks in its construction. 200,000 cubic yards of soil from adjacent cuttings were tipped to form the approach embankments. In November, heavy rain caused the River Glen to burst its banks and flood a large area of the surrounding countryside. Part of an embankment was washed away, and work was suspended for a few days, throwing a number of men out of employment. Presumably they were easily able to find alternative jobs, since a local newspaper report had recently complained about the scarcity of labour in several parts of the district because of the demand for workers on the railway, where wages were much higher than could be obtained elsewhere; a railway labourer could earn £1 a week at this time, or even 25 or 30 shillings if on piecework.

When work resumed on the viaduct, a couple of men were injured in separate accidents; a stone-mason was hit by a falling block of stone when the shear-legs of some pulley tackle collapsed, and another man had his foot crushed by the contractor's engine while engaged in shunting operations.

*The five arches of Lound viaduct, spanning the shallow valley of the Lound Beck about a mile west of Toft tunnel. (M & GN Circle)*

Further westwards, towards Little Bytham, was another major cutting, 35' deep at its maximum, which necessitated the removal of 200,000 cubic yards of spoil. Two steam navvies were employed on this at the height of operations, during the summer months, transferring the earth into wagons (about 450 loads daily), which were then hauled away by locomotives to be tipped to form embankments elsewhere along the route, mainly on the west side of Glen valley, on the approach to Lound viaduct. By the summer of 1891 work was advancing rapidly on the large cutting between Little Bytham and Castle Bytham, half a mile long and 30' deep. The underlying material here is rock, and it had to be removed by explosives; in June one navvy, Samuel Payne, was admitted to Stamford Infirmary with burns to the head and legs after injudicious use of gunpowder. A more serious accident occurred a few months later when a temporary bridge at South Witham collapsed and killed George Preston, known to all and sundry as Little Toby. By mid-1891 the number of navvies at South Witham encampment had risen to 300, which had the startling effect for the 1891 Census of trebling the village's population. Such large concentrations of brawny workers, notorious for their drunkenness, strong language and immoral behaviour, were often looked upon with consternation by the inhabitants of the areas they invaded, but there does not seem to have been any unusual amount of trouble caused by the workers anywhere along the 18 miles of this line. There were the inevitable petty crimes: navvy John Smith charged with stealing a goose, value 7/6, from the Rev. Tollemache-Tollemache, rector of South Witham, and another navvy, William Goddard, charged with receiving said stolen goose; John Williams convicted of stealing a pair of scissors and other articles, valued at 5/-, and sent to prison for 14 days hard labour; Alfred Redgrave arrested for rather uncharitably absconding with the boots belonging to his fellow-lodger Frederick Kingston; a nameless ganger who even more uncharitably ran away with the navvies' sick-club money. Perhaps the low incidence of crime was partly due to the appointment by the MR of two special constables for six months in 1891, when the number of men employed was at its highest; these gentlemen, paid 30/- a week, patrolled the workings purposefully, keeping an eye open particularly for signs of drunkenness among the workers. Early in 1892 the MR terminated their appointment on the grounds of cost; ironically a few weeks later four navvies were before the courts charged with being roaring drunk at Little Bytham.

The most serious incident concerning navvies seems to have occurred when two labourers, James Hook and Thomas Smith, met in bare-fisted combat in a field near Wymondham. The two men had quarrelled some time before in a pub in Melton, and now Hook belligerently insisted on finishing the argument. Although Smith at first refused, Hook's taunts became too much for him and the pair of them slogged it out unmercifully until Hook was felled and collapsed in the shadow of a wall; he was later found to be dead. Smith gave himself up to the police and was sent for trial on a charge of manslaughter.

The morals and behaviour of the railway labourers were a keen concern of the Navvy Mission Society, a familiar presence on any large railway working in the latter years of the century. Local Mission Rooms were set up at Little Bytham, in the Victoria Hall at Bourne, and at Castle Bytham (whose Mission was officially opened by Lady Frances Cecil), and regular meetings and "entertainments" were held; at Bourne, for example, Mr. A. Mousley, son of the contractor for that section, put together a programme of violin solos, songs and recitations at which, we are told, "the humorous element met with hearty appreciation". In May 1892 the navvies at Castle Bytham were visited by Miss Spofford, fresh from her crusading among the wild workers of the Manchester Ship Canal, and who delivered a "very earnest and powerful address" on behalf of the Christian Excavators Society, apparently listened to with rapt attention by the Castle Bytham men.

That the majority of the navvies were well behaved and accepted by the villagers of the area was nicely shown on the occasion of the Village Feast Day at South Witham in 1891. Under a blazing blue sky, and to the accompaniment of the Castle Bytham Brass Band, the navvies entered fully into the festivities, organising a tug-of-war competition between the labourers and the gangers (the labourers won), and a cricket match between the representatives of the workers on the Castle Bytham and Little Bytham stretches of line. Mr Nowell, the contractor, and his wife were there, and Nowell donated many of the prizes presented to the victorious competitors.

By now it was apparent that the suggested opening date for the line of August 1892 had been too optimistic, since much work remained to be done. More severe weather at the beginning of the year, with hard frost and heavy snowfall, put 400 men out of work and brought progress to a halt on many parts of the route. The tunnelling at Toft continued, however, and by spring of 1892 the bore was almost complete. At Castle Bytham the deep cutting through the village was pushed forward slowly; a navvy was killed in June when he was struck by the contractor's engine during soil-tipping operations. In May an impressive party of 40 directors and officials of the GNR and the MR visited Bourne to inspect the site of the new station and to finalise plans for its construction.

Although autumn of that year did not see the completion of the whole line, it had by that time reached at least an approximate state of readiness throughout most of its length. On Nowell's section between South Witham and Little Bytham, work was almost finished except for the station buildings at South Witham, which was a separate contract let to Mr. C. Barnes of Melton, who was also responsible for the stations at Wymondham and Saxby. At the western end of the line the new curve at Saxby had been opened on August 28, and the station layout extensively modified and enlarged. The 1848 station building was retained in use for handling goods, and the trackwork of the original Saxby curve was terminated at the road connecting Saxby village with Stapleford Park to form a double siding. The new station boasted three platforms, the middle one being an island, all located directly beneath a road bridge from which access was gained to the platforms by flights of steps. The most northerly platform contained the main station building, a squat, single-storey brick structure, and perhaps not particularly eye-catching or impressive, but functional enough. The shelters on the other two platforms were of wood, and made to seem rather top-heavy by the canopy roof which projected over all four sides.

By the end of 1892 a total of £52,121 had been expended on the Bourne-Saxby workings, almost £20,000 of it in the latter six months of the year. By the end of February 1893 the Midland's Chief Engineer, Mr McDonald, was reporting that 18 miles of track had now been laid, and apart from large-scale operations still continuing on Toft tunnel and Castle Bytham cutting, most of the remaining work was minor; he expected the line to be open for traffic by the middle of the year. On April 21 the directors of the GNR and the MR were able to see the progress being made when they inspected the route by riding over it in a special saloon car. On Sunday, June 4, a large gang of men was put to work making the final connections between the MR and GNR systems at Bourne and Saxby, and on the following day, June 4, the line was finally opened for goods traffic. The first train from Leicester, came through early in the morning, reaching Bourne at about 7am on its way to South Lynn yard, and in the course of the day about 30 more goods trains rattled along the new line in both directions.

From the beginning, Midlands coal was an important commodity, and the first consignment, a modest two wagon-loads, was delivered on the first day of operations at South Witham, where two coal merchants, Messrs Ellis & Everard, and T.G. Bennet of Market Overton, had already made arrangements for business at the station. By October, the daily service of trains had been supplemented by a regular nightly service of Midland goods trains running from Spalding to London via Bourne and Saxby. The gradients which west-bound trains faced out of Bourne sometimes gave trouble, and there was a period in the autumn of 1893 when a stock of poor engine coal loaded into tenders meant that several trains ran out of steam on the approach to South Witham, with consequent delay to services. The approach of winter added the problem of severe weather; in late November a ferocious gale swept the whole country, with howling winds and heavy rain; buildings were damaged, trees uprooted, and off the coast ships were sunk - 20 vessels from Grimsby alone went down, with the loss of over 50 sailors. With the approach of night the temperature fell, and the rain turned to driving snow. On the exposed heights near South Witham and Wymondham the gale-force wind blew the snow into huge drifts, and a goods train heading west into the blizzard found itself brought to a halt, trapped in an eight-foot snowbank. The breakdown gang from Melton Mowbray had to be called out and struggled for several hours in the dark and cold before they could clear the line sufficiently for the train to resume its journey.

It had been expected that passenger services would begin soon after the inauguration of goods services - the last week of July had been mentioned - and in fact a special excursion train from the Midlands to Lynn did use the route on June 25; a general passenger service was, however, postponed, presumably because of the incomplete state of the line's stations, particularly at the Bourne end, where considerable re-modelling of the station site had only just begun, the existing station facilities being insufficient to cope with the expected increase in traffic consequent on the opening of the Saxby link. That a new station was to be built here had been decided back in 1890 and originally it had been announced that the old Red Hall would be demolished to make way for the improvements. Apart from being Bourne's very first station house, the Hall was, in itself, a very historic building, and there was considerable local agitation about its impending destruction. A local architect, Mr John Traylen, of Stamford, enlisted the support of numerous tradesmen and influential members of the Bourne area in the presentation of a petition to the directors of the MR and GNR Companies which stated:

"*We the undersigned beg respectfully to approach you on the subject of the Old Hall at Bourne now used as the railway Station, in danger of being pulled down to make way for the extension of the Railway from Saxby.*

*The Old Hall is a red-brick Elizabethan Mansion with gabled roof and stone mullioned windows, once the residence of the Digby family, standing in Parklike grounds and forms one of the many interesting historical features of Bourne. The walls are thick and strong and the Roof watertight.*

*It has formed the subject of Academy pictures and is still admired, measured and sketched by students, the fine oak stair-case inside and the venerable yew tree 300 years old being objects of peculiar interest.*

*It has attracted the attention of the Society for the Protection of Ancient Buildings who unite with us in asking you to allow it to remain untouched that it may serve a useful purpose to your Company and still exercise its quiet influence as an antidote to the restless spirit of its surroundings.*

*We can ill afford to lose such picturesque and historical relics of the past and your Memorialists therefore pray that it may still be preserved to them.*"

The appeal met with widespread support among the ordinary people of Bourne and attracted the attention of most of the London and provincial daily papers; periodicals such as the "Illustrated London News" featured drawings of the Hall in their pages. Recognising the strength of local feeling, the MR and GNR finally agreed to preserve the building and restore it, using it as the station master's residence. This was a decision welcomed by the "Grantham Journal", whose correspondent waxed nostalgic about the cosy informality of the Hall's main room, which did service as the waiting-room of the old station:

"*There was always a delightful levelling of social distinctions in this dear old low-ceiled, thick-walled, rambling room. Duke and ditcher met on the same level; the invidious barriers of first, second and third class humanities were ignored. On a bitter winter day the roaring fire would be eclipsed by the opaque forms of as many honest Britons as could comfortably squeeze themselves into the charmed but limited circle.*"

*A Memorial from the Inhabitants of Bourne and Neighbourhood to the Directors of the Great Northern and Midland Railway Companies.*

*We the undersigned beg respectfully to approach you in the subject of the Old Hall at Bourne now used as the Railway Station, in danger of being pulled down to make way for the extension of the Railway from Saxby*

*The Old Hall is a red brick - Elizabethan Mansion with gabled roof and stone mullioned*

Work on the new station did not really get under way until June 1893, and entailed the building of a new goods shed and a larger, 2-road engine shed, as well as extensions to existing sidings and loading docks. The signalbox at South Street level crossing was replaced by a bigger box (a new signalbox, Bourne West, at the junction of the Saxby and Essendine lines, had been provided in time for the opening of the Saxby line). The most noticeable improvement was to the platform and station buildings. With the abandonment of Red Hall as station offices, the 1860 platform in front of that building became redundant and was removed, being replaced by two sidings; the island platform was then considerably extended, to 700', and this contained all the necessary offices: waiting rooms, porters' rooms, parcels accommodation and booking office (although this was not actually opened for business until mid-July). It was originally intended to provide a subway from the approach road to the platform, but this idea was abandoned in favour of an iron footbridge, erected by Messrs. Arnold & Son of Doncaster at the end of 1894. The whole station works cost around £25,000.

Passenger trains eventually began to run between Bourne and Saxby on May Day, Tuesday May 1, 1894. There was no official opening ceremony, but large crowds of people turned out to greet the first trains and at Wymondham the station was decorated with flags and banners. There were three trains a day each way: in the Up direction (Bourne-Saxby) arriving at Bourne from Spalding at 9.25am, 12.15pm and 5.20pm and on the Down line arriving at Bourne at 11.11am, 2.20pm and 8.25pm. Opening day was market day at Melton Mowbray, and so trains were well filled with farmers, with nearly a hundred people booked through to Melton on the first train. By July, special-rate market day tickets were made available for Leicester market, the cost from South Witham, for example, being 2/8 return.

From the beginning there was a thriving traffic to and from Spalding cattle market, held on Tuesdays; buyers of fat cattle regularly travelled from Leicester and Nottingham (an average of 250 passengers a week used the special Tuesday market trains in 1900), and the cattle themselves, herded through Spalding's main street to the station, would be loaded into cattle trains which then ran via Bourne and Saxby to the appropriate Midland stations. There was a similar weekly stock market at Bourne, on Thursdays, which also generated valuable traffic for the railway.

Other special excursions began almost immediately: early in June, Thomas Cook, the pioneering travel company, arranged an outing from Leicester to Holbeach, where a military tournament and sports events were being held. The return fare from South Witham was only 2/-, but the weather proved very unkind and only three people actually booked seats from that station. The first special train to be chartered by a private individual ran on May 24 and was used by Mr William Younger, the Unionist Parliamentary candidate for the Stamford Division, who required swift transport to take him to Melton Mowbray after a Conservative meeting in Bourne.

# CHAPTER FOUR
# THE ROUTE

The completed line, worked on the electric tablet system for the single-track section, and by block working for the double-track, was 18 miles 9 chains in length, measured between Saxby station and Bourne West Junction. The "0" milepost marking the beginning of the branch was actually located in front of Saxby Station signalbox, from where the Bourne line gradually diverged from the main Midland line, crossing the River Eye and climbing away at 1 in 100 for a mile and a half until a short level stretch was reached.

*92121 approaches Saxby station in December 1960 with an iron-stone train off the South Witham branch. On the right 8F 48361 simmers ignominiously after being derailed in the sand-drag, having passed signals at danger. Note the '0' milepost in front of the signalbox, indicating the start of the Bourne line. (H.N. James)*

A further, less severe, climb brought the line to the first of two intermediate stations, at Wymondham, 2 miles 34 chains from Saxby (the name was soon changed to Edmondthorpe & Wymondham to avoid confusion with Great

Eastern's station at Wymondham, near Norwich). Station facilities here were of reasonable provision, with a separate goods yard (capacity 23 wagons) and shed to the south of the main line, separated from the 400' - long platforms and station buildings by an overbridge carrying Butt Lane, the main road north out of the village (later changed to Station Road). The main offices were housed in a single-storey brick building in the same style as that at Saxby, located on the Down side of the 676-yard long station loop; the Down side platform also contained the small signalbox, of standard MR design.

*Intense activity at Saxby Junction: 4F 43937 brings in a Leicester to Yarmouth excursion, an iron-stone train passes on the Peterborough-Syston line, and in the background two engines are in the process of changing trains. To the right, half-hidden by smoke, is the 1848 Saxby station building, with a line of mineral wagons standing on the original Saxby curve, now a siding. (H.N. James)*

From Wymondham the line continued to climb steadily through a series of cuttings, emerging at about 5 miles from Saxby at the highest point of the route, 439' above sea level. From here it was almost all down-hill to Bourne, except for a few brief level stretches. At 6 miles 74 chains was located South Witham station, perched on a high, narrow embankment above the outskirts of the village, and this perhaps explains why the buildings and platforms were constructed of timber rather than brick, which would have needed substantial foundations difficult to provide on such a site. As at Wymondham, the platforms were 400' long; the passing loop was 279 yards, and the goods yard, also on an embankment behind the station, could hold 50 wagons.

*Station layout at Edmondthorpe & Wymondham, showing main buildings in the same style as those at Saxby, with the signalbox half-way down the platform. In the left foreground, note the rails of the steps leading down from the road bridge. (F. Church)*

*The crew of 4F 44151, heading a string of empty iron-stone wagons, bask in the sunshine at Edmondthorpe & Wymondham, waiting in the station loop to be crossed by a west-bound train. (H.N. James)*

*Bird's-eye view of South Witham Station, with its wooden platforms and station shelters. The signalbox can be seen just beyond the end of the Up platform, and to the right of the picture are the sidings and plant associated with the extensive iron-stone workings at South Witham. (Author's collection)*

*A platform-level shot of South Witham station, looking west towards Saxby, in October 1958, a few months before the withdrawal of passenger services. South Witham, however, remained as a railhead for ironstone traffic until 1964. (F. Church)*

From South Witham the line dropped through cuttings, passed underneath the Great North Road (which during construction of the overbridge, had been temporarily diverted at this point) and then through Castle Bytham village to level out again briefly at the bridge which carried the line over the Great Northern main line just north of Little Bytham station; the girder bridge was a single span of almost 100' between substantial brick abutments, and weighed 152 tons. Although the route here was still single-track, the bridge actually carried two lines, since a refuge siding, with space for 50 wagons, ran from Little Bytham signalbox for some distance west of the bridge.

The junction of the MR and M & GN Joint systems was located at 13 miles 7 chains from Saxby, near the isolated signalbox (Little Bytham Junction) of standard MR design and equipped with tablet-catching apparatus at the point where the single track diverged into double track for the rest of the distance between here and Bourne. A short distance east of Little Bytham box the line crossed by a brick bridge the old trackbed of the former Edenham-Bytham Railway, built privately by Lord Willoughby d'Eresby to serve his estates at nearby Grimsthorpe. Opened in 1857, the line was actually authorised to carry passengers, but a combination of sharp curves, rough track and unreliable motive power meant that services were rather precarious; the railway staggered on fitfully until the 1880s when it finally expired, having been reduced to using horse traction in its final years.

Skirting Dobbin's Wood, the Bourne-Saxby line curved gently into the Glen Valley, which it crossed by the Lound viaduct, longest and tallest bridge on the route, before passing under the Edenham-Toft road and reaching, at 16 miles 55 chains, the west portal of Toft tunnel. The tunnel itself was of modest dimensions, only 330 yards long, but had the distinction of being the only tunnel on the whole of the M & GN Joint system.

*The east portal of the 330-yard long Toft tunnel, the only tunnel on the whole of the M & GN system. (E.L. Back)*

At the east end, trains emerged to run downgrade at 1 in 100, through a succession of overbridges carrying lanes and footpaths, to reach Bourne West signalbox, and the junction with the Bourne-Essendine line, before the final approach to Bourne station.

*A local postcard view, dated around 1910, showing a repair gang tackling a "remarkable land slip" on the embankment approaching Lound viaduct. (M & GN Circle)*

*The Up side of the island platform at Bourne, used by most west-bound trains, photographed from the goods shed sidings. (Author's collection)*

## CASTLE BYTHAM

From the early days of the construction of the line there had been some surprise, and some concern, expressed that there was to be no station provided between Bourne and South Witham, a distance of 11 miles. At the beginning of 1892, a correspondent in the "Stamford Mercury" found the omission of the intermediate station "scarcely credible" and suggested strongly that "it would be in the interests of local trade" for the MR to modify its decision. It was true that the area between Bourne and Little Bytham was very sparsely populated, with only the very small village of Lound anywhere near the railway (Witham on the Hill, a more substantial settlement, was a good mile distant from the line) but Little Bytham and Castle Bytham had between them a population of well over a thousand and could claim to be worth the cost of a station in the amount of traffic, both goods and passenger, that they might generate. Little Bytham was, of course, already served by the GNR, and because of this the claims of the neighbouring Castle Bytham gradually gained preference. A local petition was presented to MR officials suggesting that coal traffic alone would provide sufficient business to cover costs; the point was also made that two-thirds of the business currently done at Little Bytham's GNR station came from the villages of Castle Bytham, Clipsham, Holywell and Stocken Hall, a sure indication that there was a real need for station facilities at Castle Bytham itself. Hopes were high that this petition would produce results but it was with great disappointment that the villagers heard, in May 1893, that the MR directors had turned down the idea of a station there on the grounds that, contrary to what the locals might believe, in the Midland's view the district did not possess sufficient industry, outside of agriculture, to warrant the outlay on building and staffing.

Although this was a setback, pressure continued to be put on the MR even after the line was opened for passenger traffic, and there was some excitement in September 1894 when a party of MR officials arrived to inspect the site at Castle Bytham. Maybe their business was nothing to do with thoughts of a station, or maybe their deliberations confirmed their original belief; either way, nothing came of the visit and the village had to be content to watch the trains steam through without stopping. Two years later, however, at the end of 1896, the persistence of the District Council, and of one influential member of the area, J.W.H. Davenport-Handley of Clipsham Hall, was rewarded when the MR finally agreed that there was sufficient traffic being generated along the line to warrant the addition of a station at Castle Bytham. Work began in the spring of 1897 at the chosen site, deep in the rock cutting that carried the line through the village. Because of the narrowness of the cutting at this point, the station was rather uncomfortably squeezed between track and sheer rock wall, with no room

*A shot of the wooden station building at Castle Bytham, taken from a carriage of the 10.22 am train for Bourne on December 29 1958. (M.C. Neale)*

for a yard or proper approach road; a narrow path leading steeply down from the main road gave the only access to the 300'-long platform. A goods loop was also laid to the west of the station site, with a goods shed (later removed) and a loading dock. By the middle of 1897 it looked as if work was virtually complete, and opening for traffic was confidently expected at any time; unaccountably, the MR then announced that the station would not be ready until the end of the year. It was, in fact, January 3, 1898, before the first trains called, and these were only goods trains; there were further delays in completing the passenger accommodation (a strangely prolonged process, considering the rather primitive wooden structure that did service as waiting-room and booking-office) but eventually, on April 4, passenger services began. The first train to stop there was greeted by a crowd of locals, and as it left there was, one newspaper report said, "a shout of satisfaction from the grateful villagers".

The initial service was three trains a day each way, calling at Castle Bytham from Bourne at 9.42am, 12.28pm and 5.35pm and from Saxby at 10.55am, 1.58pm and 8.00pm. Goods traffic was stimulated by the opening by a Leicester coal merchant, Joseph Boam, of a coal depot next to the goods loop and a stone quarry on the high ground opposite the station itself, with a tramway running down to the loading dock. Soon after the opening to goods traffic, it was reported that coal sold in the area was already 3/- a ton cheaper than it had been previously.

# CHAPTER FIVE

# EARLY GOODS TRAFFIC AND PASSENGER WORKINGS

From the beginning it was agriculture, as expected, that provided the Bourne-Saxby route with its staple goods traffic outwards, and this was supplemented, for a short time after the line's opening, by regular consignments of bricks from small brickworks established at either end of the route. As has already been mentioned, many of the bricks required for the construction of Lound viaduct and Toft tunnel had been produced by Kingston's of Bourne, using clay from the foot of Stamford Hill. Bourne itself stands on the western edge of a huge belt of Oxford Clay which stretches from Dorset through Bedfordshire, Cambridgeshire, and Lincolnshire to the Humber estuary, and in the late 1880s Henry Kingston had exploited this natural resource and had opened brickworks on the edge of

Bourne, a few hundred yards west of the station, near the wooden footbridge, erected later, which was known locally as the Red Steps. The opening of the Saxby line meant that the works was now conveniently sited next to the railway, which passed along the bottom of the yard, and it was a logical step for Kingston to request rail access to his premises for the easier conveyance of his bricks. By agreement of February 8, 1894, the new M & GN Joint Committee agreed to construct a single siding (known as Kingston's Siding, and worked by a 2-lever ground frame) as far as the boundary of Kingston's yard, while Kingston himself undertook to meet the cost of this construction and to provide on his own property "such other works as may be necessary to enable the works to be properly and profitably used." The siding was duly installed, and officially inspected on April 16, 1894.

By 1898 Kingston's yard had been taken over by the Bourne Brick & Tile Company (although Kingston himself was retained as manager); soon after, a rival concern, in the form of the South Lincs. Brick and Tile Company Ltd., opened on land directly adjacent to Kingston's site. Since the new Company also desired rail access, the existing single siding was modified to provide entry to both the Bourne and South Lincs. yards, while a crossover and headshunt were laid down on the main line and a small signalbox erected to control the junction (see diagram). In spite of the disappearance of his Company, Henry Kingston's name was perpetuated in that the new siding complex continued to be referred to as Kingston's Siding (as did the signalbox), even though the South Lincs. Company was served by what was officially known as Keeble's Siding. In view of the siding's proximity to Bourne station, wagons were allowed to be propelled to the site during daylight hours, provided that the front vehicle was a brake van with a guard riding in it.

The Bourne Brick & Tile Company went out of business some time just before the First World War, and on October 24, 1920, Kingston's Siding signalbox was closed, the lever frame being sent to Long Sutton station, whose signalbox was being renovated at the time. The sidings were then worked from Bourne West Box, and later, with the cessation of all brickmaking activity there, the layout was altered to a single refuge siding alongside the main line, with capacity for 50 wagons.

At the other end of the Saxby line, at Edmondthorpe & Wymondham, where a narrow belt of marlstone is present, the same Joseph Boam who had recently opened the coal yard and stone quarry at Castle Bytham's new station, developed, in 1899 or 1900, a small 2-kiln brickyard to the north of the main line and alongside a lane which became known as Brickyard Lane. A siding to serve the yard was accordingly laid in from the Up side of the station loop.

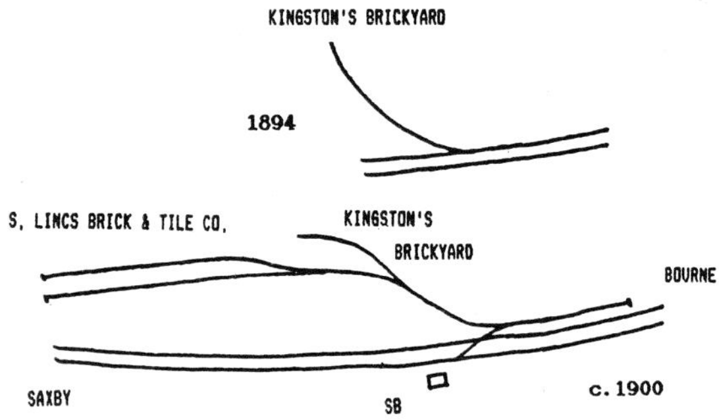


**KINGSTON'S SIDING** (From research by Graham Kenworthy)

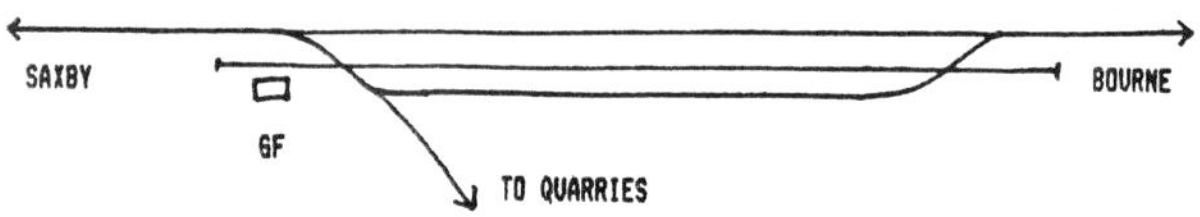


**PAIN'S SIDINGS**

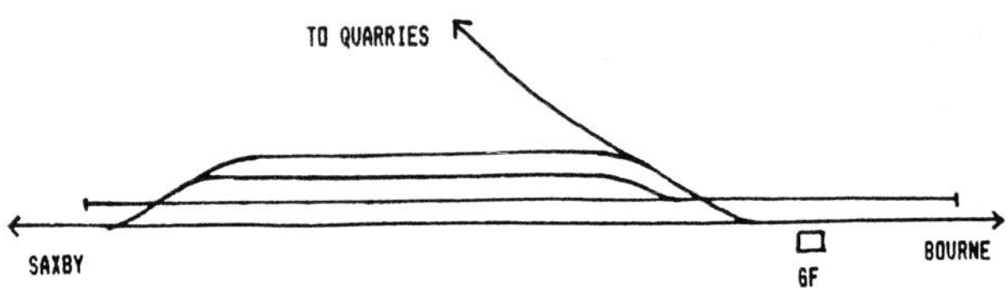


**BUCKMINSTER SIDINGS**

It was, however, the large-scale quarrying of limestone and iron ore that provided the line with outgoing traffic on a very significant scale, a traffic that lasted until closure of the whole route in the 1960s. The first workings in the area were those at Cottesmore, a few miles south of Market Overton, which were opened up in 1882, and, from 1883, served by the MR's mineral branch from Ashwell which at one stage was intended to form part of the Bourne-Saxby through route (see Chapter 1). This particular area is rich in iron ore, and the ore-bearing seams proved capable of being worked well into the 1950s, by which time an extensive system of feeder lines and tramways had been constructed, snaking its way across the countryside. It was, of course, the MR's station at Ashwell that initially dealt with all mineral traffic from this ore-field, but the opening of the Bourne-Saxby line in 1893-4 prompted further exploration and quarrying to the north of the Cottesmore workings, which eventually produced their own system of tramways and interchange sidings at various points along that route.

The first development served by the Saxby line was at South Witham, where from 1895 the staple industry was the digging of limestone, at first on a site to the east of the station. By 1907 the area immediately behind the station had been opened up, and a standard-gauge tramway (utilising second-hand rails from the recently-abandoned Kettleby mines) was laid down to bring the quarried limestone to the station sidings. Because South Witham station was on an embankment, and therefore much higher than the quarry railway, a wooden-framed hoist, with a lift operated by a gas engine, was provided to take the limestone from quarry to station level, where it was loaded by conveyor belt into waiting wagons. The original hoist was burnt down in the 1930s and replaced by a more durable steel-framed construction powered by a diesel engine. In 1944 the quarries were extended westwards towards what became known as Thistleton Mines, whose principal industry was the extraction of iron ore rather than limestone.

In 1898 the Holwell Iron Co. Ltd., who owned the original workings at South Witham, built a standard-gauge line and interchange sidings on the windy heights between Wymondham and South Witham in order to serve an extensive system of ironstone quarries being opened up around the villages of Buckminster and Sewstern. Known logically enough as the Holwell Iron Company Sidings, the three lengthy sidings (including a loop and headshunt) were located on the northern side of the Bourne-Saxby line, at 5 miles 68 chains from Saxby Junction, and could hold nearly a hundred wagons. Access to the loop was controlled by a "stage", or ground frame, operated by the train crew and released by the section tablet. In 1899 the name of the sidings was officially changed to Buckminster Sidings, which it retained until closure.

Progressive extensions to the iron-stone workings eventually meant that by 1916 the whole quarry system had been pushed far enough north for its associated tramways to make an end-on junction with the GN's recently-opened High Dyke mineral branch, which left the East Coast main line about four miles south of Grantham. In 1918 the whole of the Buckminster Quarries, together with the South Witham mines, passed into the ownership of the Stanton Ironworks Co. Ltd.
The third, and final, development of ironstone loading facilities on the Saxby line came in 1906 when, at a remote and uninhabited spot a mile west of Buckminster Sidings, at the highest point of the route, a 2-road loop and headshunt was laid to allow the interchange of wagonloads from quarries at Market Overton. Known as Pain's Sidings, after the developer James Pain, they were, like the Buckminster system, controlled by ground-frame; as with the other two systems along the route, they were also taken over by the Stanton Ironworks Company, although not until 1928.

There were special instructions for working Pain's and Buckminster Sidings, as detailed in the Midland Appendix. At Pain's no vehicles were allowed to be shunted on to the main line at the west end of the loop, where the gradient fell away to Edmonthorpe & Wymondham station, unless there was a brake van, with brakes fully applied, at the other end of the train. Trains which had proceeded to either Pain's or Buckminster Sidings for the collection or delivery of wagons were allowed to return in the direction from which they had come without going through the whole of the Edmondthorpe-South Witham tablet section.

The stone quarry at Castle Bytham, opened by James Boam, had, by the early years of this century, been taken over by Rippon's Lime and Stone Company, and was served by its own siding, with capacity for about 20 wagons.

Train services along the Bourne–Saxby route were mainly in the charge of MR engines; in the early years, for example, two Midland 0-4-4 tanks were stabled in the GN loco-shed at Spalding, together with an 0-6-0 for the through freight workings to London via Saxby. If MR locomotives worked east of Bourne they were retained overnight at South Lynn shed; for some time the local Saxby-Spalding daily passenger service (three trains each way) was worked alternately by both MR and M & GN engines on a yearly rota basis.

The passenger working that was to become known as the daily "Leicester", and which provided the line's most prestigious express service, began early in the route's history. In July 1894, only a couple of months after opening, a summer-only service of two trains east-bound and one west-bound was inaugurated to exploit the new link with the Midlands, running between Birmingham and Yarmouth, and usually conveying carriages for Norwich and Cromer, the train splitting into three sections at Melton Constable. In 1898 the service was extended to two trains in each direction, one daily, the other on Mondays, Fridays and Saturdays only, and by 1900 both trains were running daily. As they became more popular, the services were improved, with through Derby and Nottingham carriages added from the summer of 1902, which was also the year in which the service began to operate all the year round.

At first, MR engines handled the western half of the trip, changing at Bourne, but from the early years of this century M & GN locomotives (usually Johnson 4-4-0s) began to work through as far as Leicester. (This explains an unofficial M & GN designation of the train as the "Leicester", even though its destination was Birmingham; early official timetables refer to it rather more accurately as the "Birmingham Express".)

For the summer months of 1903, a through MR/M & GN service from Manchester to Yarmouth via Nottingham and Saxby was introduced, eastbound only; in the following year a balancing working appeared in the timetables.

*0-6-0 Locomotive No 92 simmers near Bourne locomotive depot. This shot was taken in 1933 and the loco' was withdrawn in 1948 (Authors collection)*

*9F 92121, a regular engine on the South Witham spur in the early 1960s, coasts past the yard at Edmondthorpe & Wymondham. The train is using the extended station loop, lengthened in the post-1948 period. (H.N. James)*

*May 1937, and LMS 2P 404 prepares to depart from Bourne's Up platform with a King's Lynn to Nottingham train. The chimneys of Red Hall are visible above the station canopy on the left. (H.C. Casserley)*

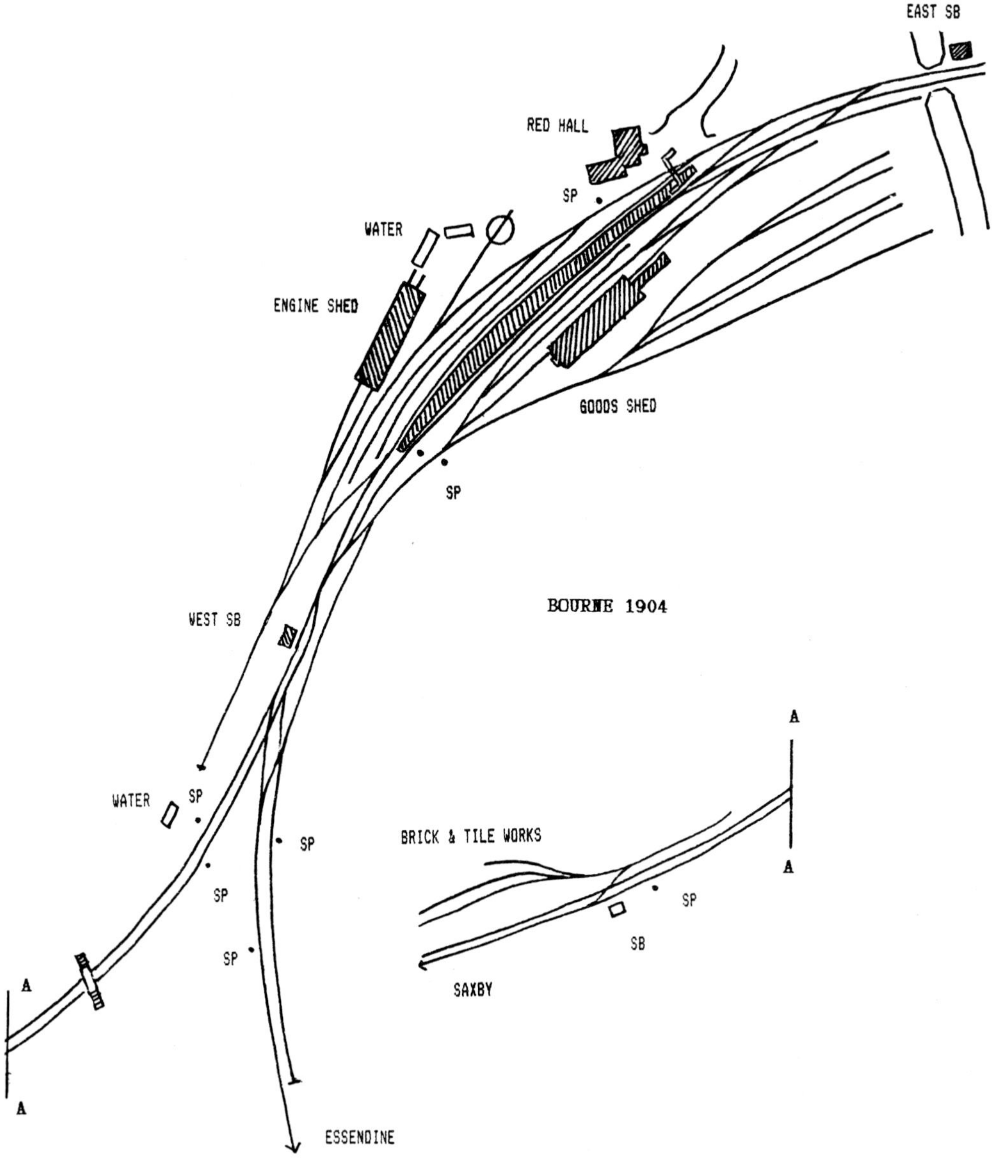
EAST SB
RED HALL
SP
WATER
ENGINE SHED
GOODS SHED
SP
BOURNE 1904
WEST SB
A
A
A
WATER
SP
SP
SP
SP
BRICK & TILE WORKS
SP
SB
SAXBY
A
A
ESSENDINE

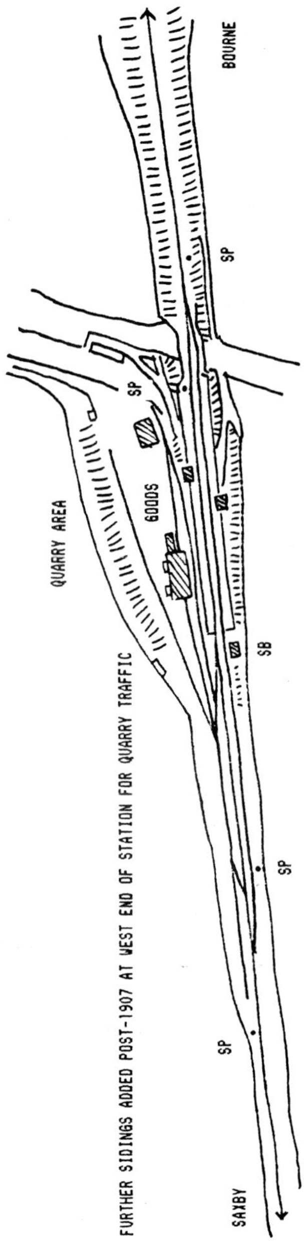


SOUTH WITHAM 1904

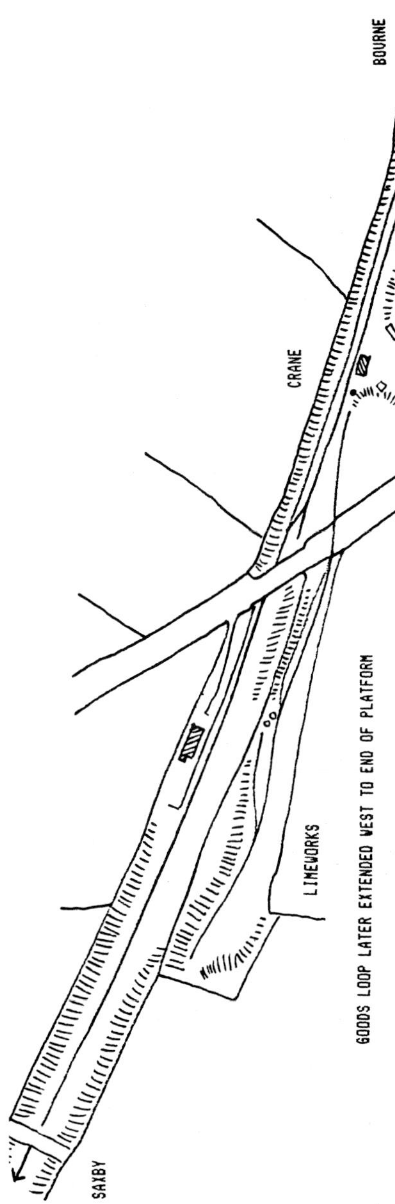


CASTLE BYTHAM 1904

# CHAPTER SIX
# DECLINE AND CLOSURE

Travelling through Kent on a Saturday afternoon in May 1939, the writer H.V. Morton was moved to comment with distaste on the change in the English countryside produced by the enormous increase in road transport:

> *"It was after the War that cheap motor-cars and motor omnibuses, and later coaches, began to transform the English road .... Inevitably the country has changed in appearance. Monotonous arterial roads take the shortest way from here to there; the petrol stations which punctuate them have developed a peculiar and horrible style of architecture which might have come from some alien planet ... I sometimes think it would be a good thing if every motor-car could be put out of action for six months to give us time to think where all this is leading us."*

Whether you agreed with Morton's strictures or not, it was impossible to deny that road transport was posing a dangerous threat to the railways as the prime mover of goods and people. Although by today's standards private car ownership was on a modest scale, it was growing rapidly, and the motor-lorry, either in the hands of the small operator or as part of a large haulage concern, was making its impact felt on goods traffic. In rural areas, however, where wages were still low, the private car was much slower to make an appearance, and in the mid-1930s there were still large numbers of people for whom the railway continued to provide the most efficient and convenient form of transport for work or leisure. It was at holiday times, particularly August Bank Holidays, that lines such as the Bourne-Saxby link were impressively busy, with dozens of extra trains ingeniously slotted into a crowded timetable, most of them conveying Midlanders from their land-locked cities to the breezy and invigorating east coast where they could sample the bracing delights of Skegness, Cromer or Yarmouth.

During the August Bank Holiday of 1936, for example, sixteen extra excursion trains were routed along the Bourne-Saxby line between 1.00am and mid-day on Saturday, August 1, most of them heading for Yarmouth and Lowestoft, but a couple diverging to Skegness, one to Mablethorpe and one to Cromer. More than half were chartered by the Leicester Co-Operative Society to take their employees from Leicester, Coalville and Nuneaton to the coast, and there was a string of relief trains later in the morning to take up any surplus. Later in the day, in the other direction, empty coaching stock was returned to various Midland stations in time for further excursions scheduled for the following Monday.

Working with such a large number of trains in addition to the regular scheduled passenger services, and along a single-line route such as the 13 miles between Saxby and Little Bytham, could produce problems for operating staff if anything went wrong, and a hold-up to one train could easily have a "knock-on" effect to following trains, particularly those scheduled to cross at stations with trains from the opposite direction. On a July Saturday in 1937, for instance, a relief express from Leicester to Yarmouth was brought to a halt between South Witham and Castle Bytham by the expiry of its engine, blocking the line for some time before an assisting engine could be sent out. Further disruption of traffic consequent on the dropping of the single-line tablet at the distant Cuckoo Junction, near Spalding, caused repercussions as far back as Saxby, where an Up express was held at the Home signal for 20 minutes, which in turn delayed the 9.10am Leicester-Peterborough train. Late in the afternoon of the same eventful day, a 15-coach train, double-headed, was held in the loop at South Witham waiting to cross with a Down train; when the latter appeared, it proved to be composed of two locomotives and 16 coaches, too long to be accommodated in the Down section of the station loop. The problem was solved by dividing the train and shunting part of it into the goods yard, thus allowing the Up train to get on its way, but by this time the scheduled timetable was in some disarray.

Apart from holiday weekends, however, passenger traffic on the railways began to decline generally in the face of increasing competition from the private car, and although the 1939-45 war, and the consequent petrol rationing, forced many people to rely on rail travel once again, the post-war period saw the downward trend accelerated. This was reflected in the reduced traffic flow along the Bourne-Saxby route; the working timetable for September 1957 to June 1958 shows just four passenger trains between Bourne and the Midlands (6.45am King's Lynn to Nottingham, which stopped briefly at Little Bytham Junction to set down or take up permanent-way patrol-men; 9.02am Yarmouth Beach to Birmingham; 4.00pm Spalding to Nottingham; 4.20pm King's Lynn to Nottingham), and four in the reverse direction (9.55am Saxby to King's Lynn, which picked up permanent-way men at Little Bytham Junction on Mondays, Wednesdays and Fridays; 1.45pm Birmingham to Yarmouth Beach; 4.20pm Nottingham to King's Lynn; 7.45pm Nottingham to Spalding). There was one Down freight, Class J, which left Saxby at 6.15pm, stopping to shunt at South Witham for 38 minutes and at Castle Bytham for 10 minutes, and arriving at Bourne at 8.12pm. A single Up freight working, originating from Yarmouth Beach at 3.35pm (3.40pm on Saturdays), went through the Bourne-Saxby section without stopping, reaching Saxby at 10.21pm

*A 3-coach Spalding to Nottingham train, with LNER D3 2128 in charge, passes the loading dock at Castle Bytham on September 27 1949. (P.H. Wells)*

By the late 1950s the Eastern Region of British Railways was sufficiently concerned about the steady loss of traffic along the M & GN route to appoint a special committee to investigate the viability of the whole line. Its report, completed in May 1958, recommended closure of almost all the 180 route miles on the grounds of declining traffic, both goods and passenger, and the costly duplication of the route by the former Great Eastern lines which, in BR's words, "parallel it across the north of East Anglia."

Because of the scale of the proposed closure, and the numerous objections lodged against it, three TUCC inquiries were necessary, held at Norwich, Peterborough and Bourne. The arguments and counter-arguments concerning the M & GN line east of Bourne are not the province of this present study - I have dealt with them in detail in an earlier book ("The Midland & Great Northern Joint Railway", Ian Allan, 1982) - and I shall accordingly concentrate here only on those points relating to the Bourne-Saxby stretch.

The TUCC inquiry at Bourne was held on October 27, 1958, when the case for retention of the rail link was put forward forcibly by Mr D. Reeson, the Clerk of the Bourne Urban Council. In essence, he made four main points.

*Bourne station on October 18 1958, with K2 61771 taking water at the west end of the platform. (F. Church)*

First, the closure of the M & GN would sever the main, and most direct, passenger rail link between the Midlands and the east coast, the connection between which areas was, it will be remembered, the main motive for the construction of the line in the first place. Secondly, the withdrawal of freight services would be detrimental to the agricultural and industrial economy of the Bourne area. Bourne was a growing town, and needed rail access; two of its other rail links had already been closed - that to Sleaford in 1930 and to Essendine in 1951 - and to remove its only remaining railway would cause considerable hardship to farmers and manufacturers who depended on the speedy and easy distribution of their products that the railway was able to offer. Thirdly, the argument that the M & GN route was duplicated by other lines was certainly not true of the Bourne-Saxby stretch, where there were no other railway lines within miles. Finally, Mr. Reeson was sceptical about the proposed substitution of bus services which, it had been suggested, would adequately bridge the gap left by the closure of the railway; these, he contended, were,

> "*to say the least, meagre in extent and frequency ... and even with the proposals put forward for new and improved bus services these services cannot take the place of the present rail services.*"

Having heard the evidence from all three inquiries, the Central TUCC issued its decision at the end of November 1958. The Bourne-Saxby stretch, like most of the rest of the M & GN route, was to lose its passenger service, although the section between Saxby and South Witham was to remain open for freight only until the remaining ironstone deposits in the area had been worked out. Bourne itself retained a goods service eastwards to Spalding, and the station also served as the collection and delivery point for the Billingborough spur, the still-operational part of the former Bourne-Sleaford route. The final day for passenger services was set for Saturday, February 28, 1959.

*On the final day of passenger operations, February 28 1959, 4MT 43060 takes the last, east-bound, "Leicester" across the girder bridge which spanned the East Coast main line at Little Bytham (P.H. Wells)*

An unusual surge of public interest in the line was evident in the final week of operations; at Saxby station, where weekly fare receipts were normally a miserable £8, more than £20 was collected, and it was reported that Edmondthorpe & Wymondham station also saw more passenger activity than it had enjoyed for some time. On the day of closure itself, various small and unofficial ceremonies were held to mark the event: at South Witham the local vicar led a congregation of about 30 parishioners onto a Saxby train, and completed a round trip by going back to South Witham immediately on the return service. For one Wymondham resident, Tommy Marriott, aged 73, whose father had been a signalman on the Bourne-Saxby line, the occasion was a unique one: as a small child he had travelled to Melton on the very first train at the opening of the line in 1894, and he ceremonially repeated this journey on the day of closure. At Castle Bytham, whose station was to close completely, the spectacle of trains blasting their way through the deep rock cutting for the last time attracted the particular attention of numerous photographers recording the day's activities for posterity.

The last Up "Leicester", hauled by 4MT 43060, and cheered on its way at the various stations en route, passed through Bourne at about 12.30 mid-day and had cleared Saxby by 1.10pm; the return working by the same locomotive, the last journey ever made by the route's crack express, reached Saxby at 3.48pm and Bourne by 4.20pm. The 7.45pm ex-Nottingham train, the very last through service on the route, carried about a hundred people (a considerable increase on normal loading), with another 20 joining the train at Saxby. Crowds of villagers at Edmondthorpe & Wymondham, South Witham and Castle Bytham, cheered and applauded as the train passed through their station and disappeared into the winter darkness. Bourne driver, Mr. S. Meeks, brought his train into his home station exactly on time at 9.04pm and completed his run a few miles further on at Spalding, reached at 9.24pm. The final train of all was a local service from Spalding, which ran into Bourne at 9.20pm.
No time was lost in putting into effect the closure of the line. On the

*A view eastwards from the road bridge at Castle Bytham, showing the weed-grown loop, crane and loading dock in June 1961. (H.N. James)*

following day, Sunday, March 1, a stop-block was erected across the line at South Witham, thus severing the route as a through link. Track was left in situ for some years, however, and it was not until the spring of 1962 that contractors moved in to lift the main line and sidings between Castle Bytham and Bourne. By October of the same year, Saxby Station signalbox had been taken out of service, and the passing loop and all sidings at Edmondthorpe & Wymondham had been removed.

The Saxby-South Witham section continued to provide regular ironstone workings, but this traffic was progressively wound down, and ceased in 1964, when Stewarts & Lloyds announced its decision to close the remaining Thistleton mines.

*The end of the line; a contractor's crane lifts track panels at Castle Bytham in the spring of 1962. (E.L. Back)*

*4MT 43066 takes the west-bound "Leicester" out of Bourne on December 29 1958. In the background are Bourne West signalbox and the Red Steps footbridge: curving away to the left the former branch to Essendine, reduced to a siding. (M.C. Neale)*

## REMAINS

It is still possible today to follow the Bourne-Saxby route for a significant proportion of its length, and to find enough of its buildings remaining to make it of interest.

At Bourne, the station site has been cleared, apart from the brick-built goods shed, which stands close by the preserved Red Hall, the original station building. A short distance out of town is Toft tunnel, and the trackbed to Lound viaduct, which is still standing but accessible only by field walking.

At Little Bytham, the girder bridge over the East Coast main line was removed in March 1964, but the brick abutments remain. Castle Bytham's station has not survived intact (apart from the dilapidated platform) although the cutting can still be viewed from the road overbridge (No. 37) in the village, and limestone working is still carried out on the site of Joseph Boam's original quarries. Amazingly, the 5-ton yard crane remains intact and rising incongruously from amongst the long grass and bushes that have overgrown the site.

At the point at which the line used to pass below the A1 road, a short length of trackbed has been utilised as a new roadway, and the original railway bridge now carries the south-bound carriageway of the Great North Road. The station at South Witham has been cleared and built over (although the underbridge is still there); further westwards is the site of Buckminster exchange sidings and the trackbed and crossing gates for the Buckminster Quarries feeder line. Ironically, quarrying has been re-started around the site of South Witham station. Pain's Siding site is still visible, although the track of the tramway leading to the quarries is now part of a private field path.

At Edmonthorpe & Wymondham the station buildings have been preserved, and renovated as a private house, and in what was the station yard are the goods shed, weighbridge office and dilapidated cattle pens.

The Peterborough-Syston route is still in operation, of course, and trains continue to pass the site of Saxby Junction. Saxby's main station building has survived, although now in rather a derelict state, but all platforms have been removed. Most durable of all, perhaps, is the station house of the original Saxby station, and, at the point where the old Saxby curve crossed the road, the old gate-house; the route of the 1848 curve is also still clearly visible.

*Sheep may safely graze ... on the trackbed of the main line through Edmondthorpe & Wymondham. Goods shed, cattle pens and loading dock are still intact in the middle of what is now a field. (Author)*

*Edmondthorpe & Wymondham station buildings, converted to a private house with a lawn and flowerbeds where the trains used to run. (Author)*

*The shell of Saxby station buildings in August 1986. The Peterborough-Syston line, still in use, can be seen in the foreground. (Author)*

## BOURNE-SAXBY : MAIN DATES

| | | |
|---|---|---|
| 1848 | May 1 | Final section of Peterborough-Syston line opened |
| 1860 | May 16 | Bourne-Essendine railway opened |
| 1866 | Aug 1 | Spalding-Bourne railway opened |
| 1872 | Jan 2 | Bourne-Sleaford railway opened |
| 1889 | June 24 | Bourne-Saxby Act sanctioned |
| 1892 | Aug 28 | New Saxby curve and station in use |
| 1893 | June 5 | Bourne-Saxby line opened for goods traffic |
| 1894 | May 1 | Bourne-Saxby line opened for passenger traffic |
| 1898 | Jan 3 | Castle Bytham station opened for goods traffic |
| | Apr 4 | Castle Bytham station opened for passenger traffic |
| | - | Holwell Iron Company Sidings (Buckminster) laid |
| 1906 | - | Pain's Sidings laid |
| 1930 | Sep 20 | Last scheduled passenger service Bourne-Sleaford |
| 1951 | June 16 | Last Scheduled passenger service Bourne-Essendine |
| 1958 | Oct 27 | TUCC Inquiry at Bourne to consider closure proposal |
| 1959 | Feb 28 | Last scheduled passenger service Bourne-Saxby |
| 1962 | - | Bourne-Castle Bytham track lifted |
| 1964 | - | Saxby-South Witham section closed |

## TICKETS

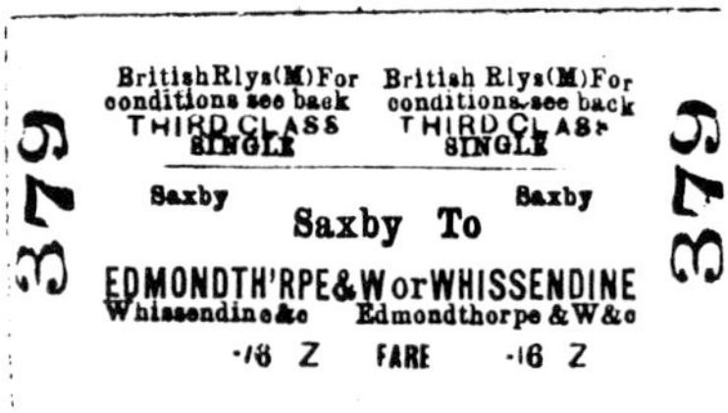
BritishRlys(M)For conditions see back
THIRD CLASS SINGLE
British Rlys(M)For conditions see back
THIRD CLASS SINGLE
Saxby
Saxby To
Saxby
EDMONDTH'RPE&W or WHISSENDINE
Whissendine&c
Edmondthorpe &W&c
FARE
379
379

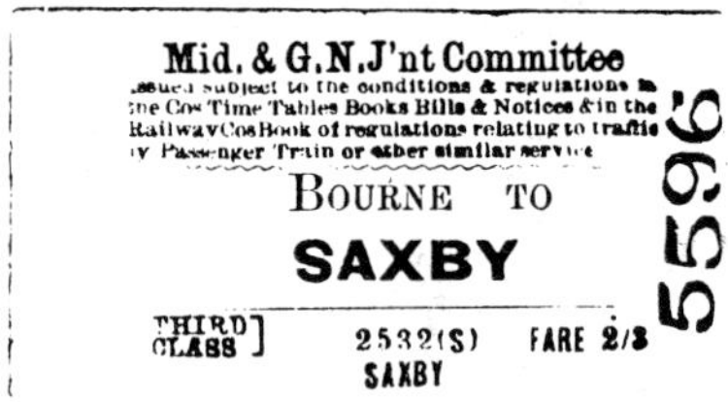
Mid. & G.N.J'nt Committee
BOURNE TO
SAXBY
THIRD CLASS
FARE 2/3
SAXBY
5596

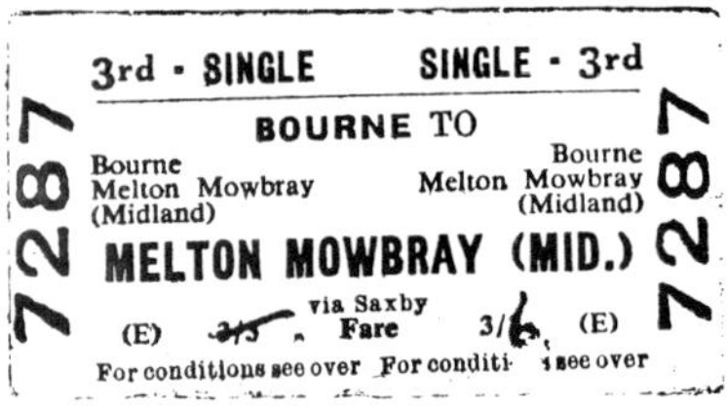
3rd - SINGLE
SINGLE - 3rd
BOURNE TO
Bourne
Melton Mowbray
(Midland)
Bourne
Melton Mowbray
(Midland)
MELTON MOWBRAY (MID.)
via Saxby
(E)
Fare
(E)
For conditions see over
7287
7287

3rd - SINGLE
SINGLE - 3rd
CASTLE BYTHAM TO
Castle Bytham
Bourne
Castle Bytham
Bourne
BOURNE
(E) 1/2 Fare 1/2 (E)
For conditions see over
For conditions see over
7435
7435

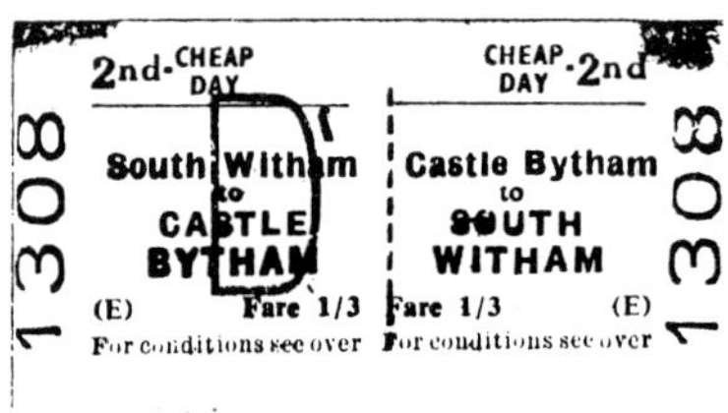
2nd-CHEAP DAY
CHEAP DAY-2nd
South Witham
to
CASTLE
BYTHAM
Castle Bytham
to
SOUTH
WITHAM
(E)
Fare 1/3
Fare 1/3
(E)
For conditions see over
For conditions see over
1308
1308

## TIMETABLES

BRADSHAW : AUGUST 1898

| Down Trains | | | A | | B | |
|---|---|---|---|---|---|---|
| BIRMINGHAM | dep | 7.50 | 9.25 | 11.15 | 2.15 | 4.50 |
| LEICESTER | | 9.35 | 10.45 | 12.50 | 3.20 | 6.25 |
| SAXBY | | 10.30 | 11.15 | 1.35 | 3.53 | 7.35 |
| EDMONDTHORPE | | 10.37 | ... | 1.40 | ... | 7.42 |
| SOUTH WITHAM | | 10.45 | ... | 1.48 | ... | 7.50 |
| CASTLE BYTHAM | | 10.55 | ... | 1.58 | ... | 8.00 |
| BOURNE | arr | 11.09 | 11.53 | 2.12 | 4.31 | 8.14 |

| Up Trains | | | | A | | B |
|---|---|---|---|---|---|---|
| BOURNE | dep | 9.29 | 12.07 | 2.30 | 5.22 | 6.20 |
| CASTLE BYTHAM | | 9.42 | 12.28 | ... | 5.35 | ... |
| SOUTH WITHAM | | 9.50 | 12.36 | ... | 5.43 | ... |
| EDMONDTHORPE | | 10.00 | 12.46 | ... | 5.53 | ... |
| SAXBY | | 10.06 | 12.52 | 3.06 | 5.59 | 6.51 |
| LEICESTER | | 11.22 | 1.47 | 3.50 | 6.50 | 7.22 |
| BIRMINGHAM | | 12.55 | 3.10 | 5.22 | 8.30 | 8.52 |

A "Birmingham Express"
B "Birmingham Express" Mon./Fri./Sat.

BRADSHAW : APRIL 1910

| Down Trains | | | | | | |
|---|---|---|---|---|---|---|
| BIRMINGHAM | dep | 8.05 | 9.50 | 1.50 | | 5.10 |
| LEICESTER | | 9.30 | 12.05 | 3.06 | | 6.43 |
| SAXBY | | 10.18 | 1.20 | 3.50 | 4.54 | 7.33 |
| EDMONDTHORPE | | 10.23 | 1.26 | ... | 5.01 | 7.39 |
| SOUTH WITHAM | | 10.31 | 1.33 | ... | 5.08 | 7.48 |
| CASTLE BYTHAM | | 10.41 | 1.44 | ... | 5.19 | 7.56 |
| BOURNE | arr | 10.55 | 1.57 | 4.20 | 5.32 | 8.10 |

| Up Trains | | | | | | |
|---|---|---|---|---|---|---|
| BOURNE | dep | 9.14 | 12.15 | 12.25 | 5.15 | 6.07 |
| CASTLE BYTHAM | | 9.28 | ... | 12.41 | 5.29 | a |
| SOUTH WITHAM | | 9.35 | ... | 12.48 | 5.37 | a |
| EDMONDTHORPE | | 9.46 | ... | 12.59 | 5.47 | a |
| SAXBY | arr | 9.51 | ... | 1.04 | 5.52 | a |
| LEICESTER | arr | 10.48 | 1.15 | 1.46 | 7.00 | 7.10 |
| BIRMINGHAM | arr | 12.58 | 3.12 | 3.12 | 8.45 | 8.45 |

a Stops to set down from beyond Bourne

## BRADSHAW : JULY 1922

| Down Trains | | | SO | SX | | SO | A | | |
|---|---|---|---|---|---|---|---|---|---|
| BIRMINGHAM | dep | 7.30 | 9.00 | 9.00 | 11.49 | | 1.55 | 1.55 | 5.15 |
| LEICESTER | | 9.06 | 10.45 | 10.45 | 1.00 | | 3.22 | 3.22 | 7.25 |
| SAXBY | | 10.01 | 11.15 | 11.25 | 1.50 | 3.50 | 4.03 | 5.11 | 8.25 |
| EDMONDTHORPE | | 10.08 | ... | ... | 1.56 | ... | ... | 5.18 | 8.31 |
| SOUTH WITHAM | | 10.20 | ... | ... | 2.05 | ... | ... | 5.27 | 8.40 |
| CASTLE BYTHAM | | 10.31 | ... | ... | 2.14 | ... | ... | 5.36 | 8.50 |
| BOURNE | arr | 10.45 | 11.50 | 12.02 | 2.27 | 4.20 | 4.35 | 5.49 | 9.03 |

| Up Trains | | | | A SX | A SO | | | | |
|---|---|---|---|---|---|---|---|---|---|
| BOURNE | dep | | 8.55 | 12.15 | 12.25 | 12.37 | 4.28 | 6.15 | 6.27 |
| CASTLE BYTHAM | | | 9.11 | ... | ... | 12.55 | 4.43 | ... | 6.44 |
| SOUTH WITHAM | | | 9.21 | ... | ... | 1.05 | ... | 6.38 | 6.56 |
| EDMONDTHORPE | | 8.15 | 9.30 | ... | ... | 1.13 | ... | ... | 7.07 |
| SAXBY | arr | 8.21 | 9.35 | 12.50 | 12.58 | 1.19 | 5.06 | 6.54 | 7.14 |
| LEICESTER | | 10.03 | 10.38 | 1.28 | 1.28 | 2.00 | 6.20 | 7.30 | 9.33 |
| BIRMINGHAM | | 11.15 | 12.43 | 2.58 | 2.58 | 3.43 | 8.46 | 9.20 | |

A - Sheringham, Cromer, Norwich, Yarmouth and Lowestoft Express

## OCTOBER 1943

Table 230 SAXBY, SOUTH WITHAM, and BOURNE

| Miles | Week Days only | | a.m | p.m |
|---|---|---|---|---|
| | Saxby | dep | 10 0 | 5 9 |
| 2½ | Edmondthorpe C | | 10 7 | 5 16 |
| 7 | South Witham | | 1019 | 5 26 |
| 13 | Castle Bytham | | 1031 | 5 35 |
| 18 | Bourne | arr | 1045 | 5 47 |

| Miles | Week Days only | | a.m | p.m |
|---|---|---|---|---|
| | Bourne | dep | 8 43 | 6 15 |
| 5 | Castle Bytham | | 8 59 | 6 31 |
| 11 | South Witham | | 9 9 | 6 42 |
| 15½ | Edmondthorpe C | | 9 18 | 6 51 |
| 18 | Saxby | arr | 9 23 | 6 56 |

C Edmondthorpe and Wymondham.

## MARCH 1954

Table 227a SAXBY, SOUTH WITHAM, and BOURNE

| Miles | Week Days only | | a.m | p.m | p.m | p.m | p.m |
|---|---|---|---|---|---|---|---|
| | Saxby | dep | 9 55 | 1 45 | 3 47 | 5 15 | 8 27 |
| 2 | Edmondthorpe & Wymondham | | 10 2 | — | — | 5 22 | — |
| 7 | South Witham | | 1012 | 2 0 | — | 5 32 | 8 42 |
| 11½ | Castle Bytham | | 1022 | 2 9 | — | 5 41 | 8 52 |
| 18½ | Bourne | arr | 1036 | 2 22 | 4 20 | 5 53 | 9 4 |

| Miles | Week Days only | | a.m | p.m | p.m | p.m | p.m |
|---|---|---|---|---|---|---|---|
| | Bourne | dep | 8 53 | 1227 | 1238 | 4 31 | 6 40 |
| 7 | Castle Bytham | | 9 11 | — | 1255 | 4 47 | 6 56 |
| 11½ | South Witham | | 9 22 | — | 1 5 | 4 57 | 7 6 |
| 16½ | Edmondthorpe & Wymondham | | 9 31 | — | .. | 5 6 | — |
| 18½ | Saxby | arr | 9 36 | 1 2 | 1 12 | 5 11 | 7 19 |

## JULY 1957

Table 231 SAXBY, SOUTH WITHAM and BOURNE

| Miles | Week Days only | | a.m S | a.m S | a.m N | a.m L | p.m | p.m N | p.m P |
|---|---|---|---|---|---|---|---|---|---|
| — | Saxby | dep | 7 44 | 9 39 | 9 55 | 1118 | 3 47 | 5 15 | 8 26 |
| 2 | Edmondthorpe & Wymondham | | .. | .. | 10 1 | .. | .. | 5 21 | .. |
| 7 | South Witham | | .. | .. | 1012 | .. | .. | 5 31 | 8 42 |
| 11½ | Castle Bytham | | .. | .. | 1021 | .. | .. | 5 40 | 8 51 |
| 18½ | Bourne | arr | 8 24 | 1017 | 1036 | 1154 | 4 20 | 5 53 | 9 4 |

| Miles | Week Days only | | a.m SN | a.m EN | a.m L | a.m S | p.m M | p.m E | p.m S | p.m S | p.m P | p.m N |
|---|---|---|---|---|---|---|---|---|---|---|---|---|
| — | Bourne | dep | 8 47 | 8 51 | 1132 | 1156 | 1222 | 1233 | 1245 | 2 55 | 4 25 | 6 42 |
| 7 | Castle Bytham | | 9 6 | 9 9 | .. | .. | .. | .. | .. | .. | 4 41 | 6 57 |
| 11½ | South Witham | | 9 17 | 9 20 | .. | .. | .. | .. | .. | .. | 4 52 | 7 9 |
| 16½ | Edmondthorpe & Wymondham | | 9 26 | 9 29 | .. | .. | .. | .. | .. | .. | 5 3 | .. |
| 18½ | Saxby | arr | 9 32 | 9 35 | 1213 | 1238 | 1 2 | 1 9 | 1 21 | 3 35 | 5 11 | 7Z22 |

E Except Saturdays
L Saturdays only. Runs until 7th September
M Saturdays only. Commences 29th June
N Through Carriages to or from Kings Lynn
P Through Carriages to or from Spalding
S Saturdays only
Z Arr 8 30 pm on Saturdays

## ACKNOWLEDGEMENTS

I would like to thank all the people who have helped me whilst writing this book, and in particular the following people for the use of their photographs

M.C. Neale
F. Church
M & GN Circle
H.C. Casserley
E.L. Back
P.H. Wells
H.N. James
Lens of Sutton

Also thank you to

The staff of the reference library at Peterborough and Stamford
The staff of the Stamford Mercury